THE OFFHAND ANGEL

THE OFFHAND ANGEL

NEW AND SELECTED POEMS

JAN OWEN

EYEWEAR PUBLISHING

First published in 2015
by Eyewear Publishing Ltd
74 Leith Mansions, Grantully Road
London W9 1LJ
United Kingdom

Typeset with graphic design by Edwin Smet
Author photograph Tennille Gibson
Printed in England by TJ International Ltd, Padstow, Cornwall

ISBN 978-1-908998-28-6

Eyewear wishes to thank Jonathan Wonham for his very generous patronage of our press; as well as our other patrons and investors who wish to remain anonymous.

WWW.EYEWEARPUBLISHING.COM

This collection is in memory of my sister
Colette Melissa Nicholson, née Sincock
(1950–2008)

JAN OWEN
is an award-winning
South Australian poet and translator
whose sixth book, *Poems 1980-2008* was published
by John Leonard Press. She was a Fellow at Hawthornden
Castle in 2009, and has participated in a number of international
poetry festivals including the Festival franco-anglais de poésie and
the Maastricht International Poetry Nights, where a
Dutch selection of her work was published by Azul Press.
Her volume of translations from Baudelaire's
Les Fleurs du Mal was published by
Arc Publications in 2015.

Table of Contents

The Kiss — 9
Young Woman Gathering Lemons — 10
Swimming Instructor — 11
The Offhand Angel — 12
The Visitation — 15
Scent Comb Spoon — 16
The Treacherous Hour — 18
Schoolgirls Rowing — 20
Sunday Chess — 22
Our Lady — 24
A Little Wine — 26
Lace — 27
First Love — 28
Kismarton — 29
Mirror Image — 30
Kohlrabi Soup — 32
Flamenco — 34
Boy with a Telescope — 35
Seascape with Young Girl — 36
The Going — 38
Touchdown — 40
Playing Ghosts — 41
The Genealogy Thing — 42
She Collected Dictionaries — 44
This Marriage — 46
The Morandi Museum — 50
The Kashan — 51
The Korin Print — 53
from *One Hundred Famous Views of Edo* — 54
White Event — 57
Optometrists on O'Connell — 58
Samovar — 60
Blue Bowl — 62
Hobart Time — 63
The Arrival — 64
Carp with Suckerfish — 65

Eating Durian with Chandra — 66
Giants — 67
Limes — 68
The Pangolins — 69
Down Jonker Street — 71
Crossing the Mekong — 72
The Wardrobe — 73
Travelling Towards the Evidence — 74
The Cut — 81
Heirlooms — 83
The Summerhouse — 85
Dividend — 86
Brownhill Creek — 87
Wings — 88
History Lessons — 89
Drawing Mermaids — 90
The Egyptian Room — 91
Ice-Oh! — 92
Climbing the Nectarine Tree at Dusk — 93
Zachary and the Angel — 94
The Trellis Fence — 96
Winter Solstice — 97
Freesias — 98
Honesty — 99
Zinnias — 101
The Irises — 102
Fern — 104
More on the Dinosaur — 105
Flittermouse — 106
Echidna — 107
On the Avenue — 108
Ibis — 109
This Instant — 111
Gnats — 114
Shifting the Dark — 115
The Bees — 116
Shingle — 120

Acknowledgements — 123

The Kiss

I love the way
a Pole will take your hand
in both of his
and straighten with the merest hint
of a military click
and bow his head
and tighten his grip
and press his moist and fervent lips
to your skin.
Also the gentle after-caress
of his moustache.
Most, I love the dark
and frankly soulful look
(still holding your hand)
he'll fix you with
for exactly three seconds after:
the look that says
this, we understand, means nothing
and everything –
  you are a stranger I salute
across the eternal silence of this space,
  you are Baila, my first love,
in her blue cotton dress,
  you are my mother
holding back her tears,
  you are garrulous Mrs Zukowski
who gave us eggs,
  you are all our grandmothers
waving after the train.
  You are woman,
we may never meet again.

Young Woman Gathering Lemons

The apronful sits on the swell of her belly,
that taut new world she merely borders now.
Above, a hundred pale suns glow;
she reaches for one more and snags her hair.
Citron, amber, white, a touch of lime:
the rind of colour cools her palm.
Extra tubes and brushes she would need –
a three in sable, or a two
should catch the gleam around each pore.
Such yellow! If there were only time.
She presses to her face
its fine sharp scent of loss
then sinks her forehead onto her wrist
– the tears drip off her chin –
till the child tugs at her dress.
She kneels to hug him close and breathe him in:
'Who's got a silly old mother, then?'
It dizzies her, the fragrance of his skin.
He nuzzles under the hair come loose.
The fallen lemons, nippled gold,
wait round them in the grass.

Swimming Instructor

for Mona Lisa in the fifth lane

Lips straight from the Quattrocento, at each end
a secret curlicue on a face as poised and round
as the smiling angel of Rheims surveying the world of men,
and a neck pure Primavera. Her green T-shirt's skin-tight
on breasts so high and full they're made to clasp.

Around her, four small boys of seven or eight
bob like apples in a barrel, shriek and splutter and gasp.
The echoes and reflections bounce off water and wall,
cross-currents of noise, drunken ripples of light.
She moves as evenly as a tide backwards along the lane,
a small head pressed against her belly, backstrokes
faltering left and right, guiding each in turn: 'Point your
toes, Michael. Head back, Luke,' she calls above the din.
Small knobs hard with cold, they flail and flounder on.

It's Sunday morning, the fathers have brought them down.
Men nearing forty now, they wait in the humid air,
fidget on benches at the side
and stare at their boisterous offspring and at her.
Their thoughts lap round like water, aching to touch,
as each little boy splashes towards horizons
green as promises, ripe as pippins in May.

The lesson done, they sigh and look away
from the bosom by Rubens under the shirt by Sportsgirl.
That smile by Leonardo's half innocent of it all.

The Offhand Angel

Five haloed numbers on her angel chart
are guarding the stick-figure self
at elbow, neck and knee.
Clashing symbols, she calls them,
wondering about the sixth
drawn-in a short way off.
Is he a sort of spare? She feels ignored.

He's a recent graduate in fact,
with a nose for chaos design.
His Endlessness typecast him
avant-garde of truth with a foot in the dark,
edgy expatriate of yes:
There is this matter called poetry down there.
More a silver excavation, a promising space.
And he is clearly to be shortfall's volunteer,
a sort of default button they call the Muse.

Go to it. He hangs around a while
regaining the knack, language is tricky
as fuzzy maths or that slant love of theirs –
a desolation blooming into light,
a Dis solution homing into night.
He must flatten, particulate, to the linear trip:

Taste, he tries, gathering presence,
(it still tastes inside out) then *Touch* –
as a tangent to a circle?
He'd sing a site of reason, colour of rhyme
but human energy tips and skews;
the nearest he can come
is a nudge of silence challenging words,
those coupling atavisms once his own.

He cancels distance now,
translated through her breath
down to that instinct they call art.
Purpose comes clear and *Birth*.
He glances in, wings her with doubt,
the shadow of a poem.
'Golden pollen' is all she scribbles.
Her scent annoys him, and her hair.

That sideways look. Has she guessed they are
the Absolute's garbage recycling team?
Almost. 'The scavenging angel sifting
the detritus for truth,' she writes.
Delete! '*of* truth.' He's moved a little nearer.
Will some of the dust rub off on her?
she wonders if he wonders.

Humour's a balancing game
that even angels play, as humans conjure
wings in a likely wind:
Is this being a metaphor? he sends.
'Is this metaphor a being ?' she writes.
She can almost see him now –
a milkiness against the sky;
words move between them like a tide.

You are amateurs of mix and match
though ingenious, smiles into her.
Ants and midges, he adds.
'Heavenly hiccups!' she replies.
Her strange attractor patterns
praise with blame: *Clumsy with hope,*
touch-centred, sniping at fate!
'Recurrence squandering its last chance,'
she agrees. 'What's more, Wailing
and Gnashing of Teeth. Right?'

But every hair of your head, he reminds her.
'Time is our spirit fasting, then?'
A bead of sweat on your lip, he whispers,
leaning close. 'Ah, feathers of sun!'
Wrong side of laughter (teasing her).
'Come through,' she says, 'Come in.'

The Visitation

No angel has descended here.
Only the woman's shining hair
shows feather soft beneath the wings
of a white starched cap whose ribbon clings,
looped in a Moebius strip of faith,
transparently against black cloth.

She's leaning right so we centre on
the outstretched arms of her firstborn;
the solid hands of the two-year-old
are flat on hers in the pat-a-cake hold.
It's a medical photograph without
the faces of mother and child blocked out.
We guess from her bewildered eyes
before we read and realise –
Six-fingered dwarfism: Amish boy
with Ellis-van Creveld syndrome. Why
this should be, his mother's ceased to ask,
but takes this witness as her task,
shuts the Book, fastens her cap,
lifts the baby onto her lap.
A certain beauty lights them both –
this trust unveiling all the truth
hallows them brightly as any Raphael
Madonna and Child. Sad and still,
her look cuts to the quick of now;
his, searches stolidly past as though
half sizing up all that's to come.

So steadily, they stare down time.

Scent Comb Spoon

Even the might-have-been returns.
The simplest thing – scent, comb, spoon –
and it swings back, streaming bright dust toward the sun,
an abandoned chaos that needs to be known,
an insistence thirsty for history, hungry for soul.
He writes the idea down,

remembering how they watched two otters once –
that sinuous skein more fluid than water itself.
Do thought and feeling twine like that,
a spiral helix speeding time?
Now the water has calmed,
reflection and loss keep faith.

But where does it go to really, he wonders,
or come back from;
is this all resurrection means,
a flicker of cells, a taste for symmetry?
Drop a dimension, and what was it all about?
His irony's nervous tic is a grey shortcut:

two hesitations *er er*
in a declaration of love,
the question/answer in a mock debate,
or less, the single quote marks either end
of an anecdote with a lame punch line –
'two dark wings that could not lift our bird to flight'.

And the joint citation for commonsense,
was it conscience, confusion, or cowardice?
Music vanishes into itself, he writes,
Words swim back through words, things of that sort.
He's writing a book on Scythia.
They say she's taken up golf.

What's left? A taste for blue.
And a keepsake to outlast them both –
the mid-month moon lugging its unseen half
like cherished flesh. There is
a wholeness to almost everything.

The Treacherous Hour
The Pyrenees Highway, Victoria

Colours are questioning the night.
A dam's sheet metal.
Now is a foreign land,
pure direction between
the fiery markers and the dotted line.
Brief as smears,
the small towns seem misspelt:
Moolort, Bung Bong.
The local signs say
Cemetery Road, Madman's Lane,
Nowhere Creek 2 km.

I have been East
to read the books of friends.
Passing the power lines at the city fringe,
I thought of their solid bodies,
the particular smell of their skin.
The forked pylons
that shoulder the lines
stride the countryside like Siamese twins.
Something I read has thumbed a ride,
is making a home from home –
at the autopsy in 1951
of a hydrocephalic child,
five foetuses were found
nested in the swollen head
of their stillborn brother
as in a womb.
Little shadows come in from the cold.

Possibility's strangest music
fills my head.
The derivation of 'monster'
is 'show, portend, warn.'
Darkness is rising now;
I ease my speed,
bearing my friends in mind.
I do not know what world I am within.

Schoolgirls Rowing

Five twelve-year-olds in short white skirts,
skinny, long-legged, filling out
but chattering with treble voices still,
are teetering over the edge of adolescence
and the slender yellow boat.

'Sir!' says blonde bunches,'What are we 'sposed to do?
There's water up to the clogs. It's practically full!'
'It's disgusting, Sir,' adds brown plaits,
'How are we 'sposed to row?'
'Shut up, girls,' the coach says, 'and get out.'

The *Dickie Richards*, with due fuss, is turned and drained.
Smiling now, back in, they push off well.
'Square your blade, Four,' says the cox,
'I keep telling you, Danielle!'
Coincidence or foul play from Prince's passing by

sends duckweed and a snigger or two their way.
'Don't buck your oar, Jane,' calls the coach.
'Kim, you're taking too much reach,
and watch that feathering height!'
As Saint's, shipshape in white and gold,

draw level in the *Piping Shrike*,
their number three looks sideways, washing out;
they steer right through the weed.
The girls stay straight-faced, lift their chins
and pull more smoothly with each stroke;

sleekly the *Dickie Richards* cuts the murky green.
Past the boys and under the bridge
skim Alison, Danielle, Rebecca, Kim and Jane;

the ripples in their wake touch *Popeye*
at the river's edge with alpha waves of light.

You're on the bank, just sitting in the sun,
but suddenly happiness has you by the throat.

Sunday Chess

The Luxembourg Gardens, Paris

I turn a corner: under the leaf-hushed birds
and the plane trees' shifting green is a deeper stillness,
fifteen couples sculpting thought
at fifteen tables spread out over the gravel,
with loiterers behind this game or that.
It's a festival of gentle breath and touch:
a black queen glissades into the sun,
a white knight leaps off into the dark,
a left forefinger clicks a timer down.
Sighs, syllables, shifting of feet; the young boy
castles his king, the grandfather taps a pawn.

I can't follow this latticework of plot
that sets off like a poem towards defeat –
two couplets sight-rhymed abba
till free verse rules with heavy editing –
so I watch the watchers
tender their intimate ironies and nods:
He'd better watch that rook.
She's moving into check.
Taming win and lose may yet translate
to worldspeak: *shah mat* – peace, brother.
And makeshift doves there are:

the pigeons underfoot, silly with doughnut crumbs
in the stretched-out silence between the moves
whose black and white will never bleed to grey
like the sleek and easy compromise of the birds –
momentary rainbows, permanent lice.
They startle up in a wave – *mouchoirs!*
then sink down by the Grand Bassin

where a squabble of children tilt on the rim,
stretching their sticks to the little yachts.
No, yours is the orange one. Maman, Maman,
Françoise is trying to push me in!

Prodded, capsized, righted, the one-wing butterflies
drift to the bright hour's endgame,
one last moment clutched against blue cloth.
And that's the feeling of being small:
the slow relinquishing of the dripping boat
for the promised *glace*, left hand clasped,
the slow scuff-scrunch of best lace-ups
under a high curved ceiling of green
past everything yet to come, the grown-up game
which is for some reason already, here and there,
packing away its men and easing back a chair.

Our Lady

Notre-Dame, Paris

She was sitting one row in front, to my right,
oddly angular in a bright red dress.

In that ornate half-dark, stained shards
of lucent rose, azure, emerald and gold

melted down through the air
and over the heads and tiles like angels' blood.

She was weeping silently, eyes fixed on the altar:
not crying, weeping, that slower, fuller grief

as river is to rain. And rivulets were coursing down
through her thick and careful make-up

so the close-shaved stubble showed
like tiny wounds. Or splinters of wood.

One way to bear your cross. If the soul descends
from truth it is male and female, turn and turn about,

with all its disguises and dishevelments
so lightly worn it is the world you had

before your face was born.
She blew her nose, and stood with us and sang:

the organ notes and colours streaming down
were throwbacks to the muted light,

paths diverging to rejoin. I followed him out
thinking to say *Très chic, Madame*

(while meaning brave), but lost her in the crowd
and sat down on the low brick wall

fifteen metres from the portico
by a crisp little hedge just in front

of a cobblestone carved MARGUERITE.
I've no idea why or who. For whom.

A Little Wine

I remember you, Dario,
courteous, long-faced croupier
who found me lost in the mist
on Verona's vast piazza
with twilight rising from the cobbles,
and how you escorted me back
through the blurred grid of alleys
towards my door, unsmiling
– yes, perfectly poker-faced –
but stopping on the way
'*per un bicchiere di vino*?'
at the counter of a small cantina
walled with bottles, a cellar come up for air.
And how a hand glanced off the lampshade
so it swayed just over the heads
of a dozen strangers like a benediction.
So the red wine, held up, sparkled on and off
and the warm Italian vowels
circled below the moving halo of light
around the invisible centre
of which we were
that moment, the tangible signs.

Lace

Scuola Merletti di Burano

Seven women facing the window light
over their *tombolini:* call it soul-work,
this patient patterning of air with white.
Care is the common angle of their neck.

The stuff's so fine their fingers strain to see.
In fact, the craft may have their eyes.
Si, siamo contente, says Paola, showing me
her Punto Venezia leaves and butterflies.

From the leaning tower, San Martino's bells
cast out their net – a silvery lace
trembles down Via Galuppi past the School.
The tiny and the immense touch and pass.

They don't look up. I pause in the narrow hall
saying *toccata, toccata*. Around the first bend –
a clothesline propped along a lilac wall:
the dancing clothes scallop the edge of the wind.

First Love

Titian's The Man with Grey Eyes, *circa 1540–45*

It happened in Physics,
reading a library art book under the desk,
(the lesson was Archimedes in the bath)
I turned a page and fell
for an older man, and anonymous at that,
hardly ideal –
he was four hundred and forty,
I was fourteen.
Eureka! streaked each thought
(I prayed no one would hear)
and Paradise all term
was page 179
(I prayed no one would guess).
Of course
my fingers, sticky with toffee and bliss,
failed to entice him from his century;
his cool grey stare
fastened me firmly in mine.
I got six overdues,
suspension of borrowing rights
and a D in Physics,
but had by heart what Archimedes proves.
Ten years later, I married:
a European with cool grey eyes,
a moustache,
pigskin gloves.

Kismarton
for Balázs

The alliance was uneasy even then.
Close to the border we found that day
your country as it was before the war
renamed Kismarton 'Eisenstadt.'
Arched doors and gateways, fruit trees,
angular houses, plain or baroque as clouds,
Eszterházy Palace where Haydn played,
and Liszt in the Square, elegant even in stone.
In the little cake shop where you bought
the cakes of your childhood,
almás rétes, pózsónyi kifli,
they spoke the old tongue still,
only you paid in schillings not in forint.
'Köszönöm szépen,'
smiled the broad-cheeked woman.
The nearby church was a simple dome,
a beehive of russet shadows and yellow light
round and warm as a country stove,
homely enough for a child to believe in God.
The sky was open as the *Alföld*.
We sat on a wall to eat.
'Look:'
a walnut tree by a barn, a wooden cart,
geese honking through wet grass
and an arc of rainbow in bruised light.
'Hungary.'
You could not swallow,
staring along the fault line of a dream.
Hungary. As close as we ever came.

Mirror Image

'Twenty-nine years ago. And only yesterday,'
says Balázs, slapping at a fly.
We sit beside a bottle underneath his vines
and watch the football arc between our sons.

'Check through the corner one,' the sergeant says,
'and make it short and sweet. Take a couple of men.'
(Seventeen-year-olds still nervous with a gun.)
It's an office block like most
down the derelict street;
he keeps a good five metres ahead,
tries the rooms along each corridor
and beckons the two boys on.
They reach the third floor,
breathing easier now.
The Council Chamber's here,
empty but for a tangle of chairs
at the northern window end
(unseemly three-day corpses,
wooden legs in the air);
dried into the floor – blood stains;
and seeping through the shattered panes
the distant dialogue of crossfire.
Directly opposite him – another door.
He notes the fact an instant before
it opens sharply and his counterpart –
the hated AVO uniform of green –
levels his gun and time is not.
They freeze. Somewhere beyond,
the seconds slide away;
between their eyes the slender lifeline holds
across the mirror of air.
'Döntetlen, barátom, azt hiszem':
Stalemate, I think, my friend.

Each slightly lowers his gun
and slowly, eyes still locked, takes one step back.
The two doors close together, softly as hands on a prayer.
'*Senki sincs ott*,' each says to his men:
Nobody there.

'In Hungary we used to say
Néha a második alkalom jön először –
sometimes the second chance comes first.'
He's silent, years away.
The day is insubstantial, seems to float
in the dry gum-scented heat.
Only the football's thud,
steady as the beat of some huge heart,
holds us in time and space.
He rouses himself to swear:
'*Az anyád*, off the kohlrabi, *rossz gyerekek*,'
then pours us another beer.
The head on each glass whispers small talk;
we blow the froth into the air.

Kohlrabi Soup

How it trapped the dust,
the stucco façade of that old square house
the colour of deepest heaven
behind the oleander's poisonous pink.
Half the backyard was an offering of scarlet tulips
like a ritual letting of blood.
In the other bed, the lymph-coloured kohlrabi
craned on their purple stalks,
slowly gathering the will to walk.

The father, young and newly ill, had begun
in desperation to build a catamaran
safe outside in the shed.
By five pm, the hemmed-in kitchen was already dim.
She had finally made him the kohlrabi soup
and put it to cool on the bench.
When he came inside,
the babies, latched in their chairs,
were brandishing spoons and shrilling with hunger;
he yanked the plug
of the bakelite radio blaring against the din
and cut the cord with his knife.

Late that night she tiptoed into the kitchen:
the abandoned soup had set to a sinister pond
gravelly-soft as semolina, elastic as phlegm.
It was the exact colour, she saw, of the moonlight
mottling the yard of scattered toys
and the phalanx of triffids beginning to stir.

Over the scene,
a disappointment balloon was drifting
to if and when
the boat would be launched,
the family split,
and the small blue house knocked down.

Flamenco

i.m. B.B.

Slipping the LP from its mildewed sleeve
I'm carried away by the smell of sadness
the must of memory
an odour of Spain's cathedrals   Granada's caves

I'm lifted by the ritual of the lowering needle
the sinew of the sudden notes'
pure religion of sound
and the voice hoarding its emptiness   the space   where joy once was
with the heels insistently going nowhere on and on
a regiment of raindrops
or heartbeats squandering love

I'm summoned back through the silence   to apse and nave and crypt
to the ones we were   still side by side
with hosts of tiny standing waves
trembling here and there in the stony dark
as we fixed our flickering tapers   onto a half-filled stand
dead centre   with the arrogance of youth
and breathed the weeping tallow smell

Burgos it was   with all we never said   of fear   purpose   hope
or patience even   the candle bundles waiting
prone and pale   bodies stacked for burning
while the sibilant lit multitudes
stretched heavenward in rags of fire

Boy with a Telescope
for Andrew

Shadowy neanderthal, his silhouette
straightens to shake a fist
at the prowling clouds,
then down again eagerly
to Saturn's swirling rings
or Jupiter trailing his brood of moons.
The warm room of the family
is galaxies away;
tonight he charts the distance and the dark,
burning with a cool celestial fire.
Names like charms spin in his head –
Betelgeuse, Rigel, Aldebaran –
they peal like bells in the cold air.
He calls me over to see
a globular cluster in Scorpius.
I squinch my face against metal,
admire a blur:
'No, no, through the secondary lens down here.'
He puts me in focus. I crouch to a pinpoint.
'Seven thousand two hundred light years away!'
He reels it off with awe.
The immensity of the night,
these tiny sparks taken on trust, we share.
I touch his arm and go,
but look back from the door:
he is swivelling to another constellation,
checking the finder, muttering to himself.
And may he always stand so –
a little to one side of what he loves,
earn a clear view
through fine adjustments, steady care.
I wish him distance and desire,
quick hands, keen eyes –
may his mind reach, tactile as fingertips,
to the sharp braille of the skies.

Seascape with Young Girl

For Eve-Marie

The heat seethes dragonflies,
their sheen, the exact colour of flight;
pink orchids stretch on wispy stems
not-quite rope tricks.

She pauses for a moment on the path
where tangled tea trees shine
with old man's beard;
two skinks glissando through her hands,
and a stumpy tail, lichen-patched, in the sun,
recognizes her with a long Jurassic gaze.

She thuds at any hidden snake
and a pair of blue wrens split the air,
splice it up, disappear.

At last – a spill of sand,
the first steep slope, a slap of wind
and before her the smiling sea.
Left and right, the dunes loll,
lion-coloured. Below,
the light bleeds silver on water;
a rainbow sail windsurfs the inshore green
and cries of gulls and children thin into air,
pure as the notes of a pipe.

Suddenly, on the next knoll in one quick leap,
there's a boy – slanting eyes, curly hair:
capering, he slings a stone,
whistles and swoops and rolls and will be seen.
Her eyes fine to horizons,
the line of her throat and chin
is smooth as the headland and as remote;

she will not notice him.
And just as suddenly, he's gone.
Her neck acknowledges an absence.

The rainbow sail is down;
wavelets fawn, bright fanged, on the beach;
the day's a haze of white noise,
tinnitus of tomorrow.
Everything's far away,
is within reach.

The Going

Bowl

The Tao of forgetting is just
pure emptiness held in trust
but lifting a little transparency from blue
to farewell sadness.
Forgetting even forgetting.

Did I honour her enough
casting off the cliff edge of each moment
or ditched on the nowhere shore
with scrambled coordinates and fading maps
my mother, going somehow on?

Her afterimage seems a space
where nothing is and yet may be:
the shape of welcome in her favourite bowl
the taupe of deep old water
round the sides and lapping over the rim

like running your mind along a secret
tropic and tasting dusk.
Inside, a scoop of glossy azure pools to
midnight blue with scattered flecks of gold
a galaxy, a future in the past.

The glaze that makes a mirror of this sky
is crazed with hairline cracks – the precipitate
birth of an archipelago
its shimmer of tiny islands losing touch
like thought marooned from thought

a thousand times a day
and listening into the silence for itself...
Near-death she'd met when young as golden light
beyond the darkness closing in:
these constellations letting go, speeding apart.

Violin

Although
there was another presence moving in at first
very quiet and long ago like a child puzzling
a theorem out as the door shut.

Maybe is the softest wind
but a sharper shrift of soon
was sifting light to salvage
hope centripetal as the simplest flower
yet lavish with scraps of love:
her violin notes remembering themselves
her touch disarming frowns.

An endless body of music was being
jettisoned and the lookout fires doused one by one
all outer provinces closed down
silence shifted to indigo. When I turned away
I was silhouette she readily forgave.

What is doubt holding itself in doubt?
She had such grace, going
and the clearest smile, shyly asking my name.
When laughter left, dance drew her in –
the last light traces lifted her hands
with their loosening rings.

Courtesy stayed and stayed
breathing her perfume into the darkening room:
Ma Griffe. Its cypress tip here at my throat
remembers where she's gone and goes there.

Touchdown

And so it comes to me now,
this small gold grub with ruby eyes,
its owner finally down after a lonely fall –
Flight Sergeant John Barnes Sincock, Navigator,
a member of the Caterpillar Club,
having saved his life by parachute.
I trace the pin latched on blue velvet
and think, too, of the wireless operator –
Vern Scheldt, twenty-two, who did not quite
qualify for the Club
but lived with us ever after
in a frame on the mantelpiece.
I was five years old
when his mother and sister came with gifts,
the portrait and a lilac poetry book.
Every Sunday as I read,
his face looked wistfully down at me,
changing with the years
from my father's friend
to a fair young man,
a youth, a boy, then my lost counterpart.
Today he could be my son.
Little remains – his smile,
remembered rhymes,
a rush of space to cross.
Now a single thought encompasses them
both safe down.
All distance closes in the end.
Already as I reach out, Vern,
I can almost touch your hand.

Playing Ghosts

As the clouds pass on,
my ceiling warms, expanding in the sun;
the pinewood fibres sing of xylem and phloem
in the flat half-notes of wooden birds
as if the passed-down cuckoo clock had lost its wits.
Memory's tapping from another room
like children in an attic playing ghosts –
that tiptoe creak, a death tick
from an older house (D sharp, G flat):
grandfather hammering in a nail,
grandmother clicking her thimble on the scissors,
stitches across worn time.
Now a laugh's staccato run, quick steps on gravel,
the whap of a tennis ball
and a crackling in the grate as the fire purrs –
they've no idea I'm gone.
All the littlest labours of rift and join are
holding my now, my then,
in this honeywood sky under the fitful sun.
I am learning world-word,
silence cradling touch:
needle-thin, the solitaries dance,
a snap of castanets, toy sounds
that make the moment home
as climbing to the attic hallowed the stair.
Flat on my back on the floor,
fronting this conversation of gold
– tree talk, sun song, sound braille,
I'm tracing the pattern of knot and grain,
pinpointing the fibre cries like secret stars,
plotting those constellations of praise and pain.

The Genealogy Thing
for Fleur

I too went searching out my forbears. In grave-high grass
in the town of their setting forth which needs a line of its own,
Llanfairpwllgwyngyllgogerychwyrndrobwllllantysiliogogogoch,
and reading the title pages of lives cut short like LlanfairPG,
wondering were these mine: Bronwyn, Hannah, Jane.
Any Thomas Owen might have a claim to be
one of the master mariners who sailed my line two centuries
from the chapel of Saint Tysilio becalmed in a sea of green.

There was nothing that tallied, no twitch of yes,
though we scoured the miniature island of names and dates
till a nuggety little man arrived with arms outspread
and led us into his square-cut gem:
slate tiles, dark stone, pale diamonds of light,
and an altar cloth with an edge like searching fingertips
or white spume off a North Atlantic wind sharpening its grudge
against grey sky and all the tall ships finally scuttled or wrecked.

Was it something in the blood, a habit of risk,
that drove my people ahead of themselves
on a clipper running before the wind or a tanker out of Liverpool
– a leaning to exile or otherness, heresy's short cut?
I think of Baruch Spinoza at his bench, grinding the lens
of speculation, fining light and colour down
till clarity's dust sifted into his lungs like scales from the eyes of God.
And what remains of that thought but extension?

What remains? From the distaff side: folding pince-nez, left lens missing,
two dented lockets, Welsh hymn book. From the spear side: watch chain,
pearl-handled pocket knife and, black-bound in a cover case,
bills of lading on flimsy paper with this slant hand like sepia lace
or faded waves on the fantasy fringe of tattered maps.

The signature is *Griffith Owen*, my great-grandfather
who died at sea. Maybe he slid shipshape into a glassy calm,
maybe they brought him home for burial in firm earth. He is not here.

Most memory is underwater, undergound. At best, refracted light.
And any family traced might be a treatise on the rainbow.

She Collected Dictionaries

as other women take up men
and shelve them:
manuals, grammars, *Teach Yourself*
German, Malay, Italian, Swahili, Welsh,
like a passion for clothes that would hang
unworn in the dark,
for peridots, garnets, amethysts, pearls
in a shut case, nouns declined.
Each unknown word shone with delicious fire
and the alien phrases silked her skin
with their genders and connotations.

She might have been the end house
on the waterfront of Macau
welcoming every sailor in.
But the longing for many tongues
to part her lips – si, igen, ya,
ah oui, yes, yes –
was departure's smile,
a leaning to the wind
that sweeps a glitter of light
across the sea and sets a silvery chill
at the neck. Quick, to those books
guarding the mantelpiece,
derivations snug as a span of days,
to bread and fruit and sparkling wine.

She had been given a cyclamen with scent,
some new trick that married violet and rose,
as if a flower should yearn to sing
and the pink timbre tremble
into quietest words.
She touched her flesh and knew
that it would fade as speech did
and did not.

And yet it was not language that she sought,
nor the music of any meaning.
An old allegiance drew her on
beyond the first ground of thought
and the idea even of silence
to the fifth season which must at last return
with its weather of recognition
and its lost ends.

This Marriage

The Well

After the angel had been
and her father's first anger was done,
she left her mother wringing
a chicken's neck, tight-lipped,
and sank down by the courtyard vine
and felt her gorge rise up.
She had half forgotten the light.
Here, only her queasy heart
like a flapping wing,
feathers filling the air
with a warm bird smell,
and the dull weight at her core.
She leant on the trunk of the vine
hard as the sinews of her fathers
till the sickness passed
then pulled herself up
and took the two buckets,
the new one Joseph had made
and the rickety one with the handle worn.
On the path to the well
the fallen olives
purpled her sandals with their stain.

Straw

Joseph stayed unsure
in spite of the dream.
When the pains began
she was calm as the oxen in their stalls
who shifted and sighed and knew.
He was afraid. This was women's work.
Somehow he got a fire going, and water warmed.

In the end it was easier than he thought,
the boy slipped into his hands
neat as a trout
and blinked at the stable's dim gold world.
He washed and swaddled him
and put him to Mary's breast.
Then remembered the afterbirth
in the straw somewhere
and carried it out and fed the fire.
He was washing his hands
when the shepherds came,
two dumbstruck men and a boy with a lamb,
a gift, they said, for the newborn lord,
wiping away all doubt
with this odd hurt –
the heavenly hosts had not appeared to him.
He bowed his head and led the strangers in.

The Blue Gown

And when the time had elapsed
and the day come
that he might go to her,
she rubbed myrrh on her throat,
touched cinnamon to her tongue,
and hung between her breasts
a silver amulet of snakes entwined
then lit three candles on a low pine stool
and loosened the cord
of the gown her mother stitched
against this night.
He drew aside the brocade,
standing a little uncertain,
a quiet stranger
who'd washed her bloodied thighs
and seen her milk well up.

She let her gown slip to a pool,
in duty and gratitude she would have said.
But when he drew his clothes off awkwardly
and she saw him for the first time,
quite unexpectedly she ran and knelt
and pressed her cheek to his skin
and circled him with her arms.
His hardness at her bosom and neck
was a curious creature
she could rouse and tame
now that her body was her own.
His hands like promises
were lifting her hair.

Leaves

It was bright moonlight.
In another room the boy awoke
and quietly lay and sucked his fist.
He heard a night bird call,
the scritch of a beetle,
the scrabble of a mouse.
He could not know yet who he was
but watched the fig tree cast
its pattern on an inner wall
and studied the light and shadow
in his father's house.

The Pomegranate Tree

The second time,
a midwife hustled the man
straight out into the yard.
He sat in the shed
with the planed wood round his feet

and the shavings' tight blond curls
till the woman's triumphant shrill.
When Mary was asleep
he took the child up in his coat
doubled against the wind
and went out to the pomegranate
heavy with open fruit
and watched the sun go down,
bending his head to catch
the sure breath of this infant,
mortal and his own.

The Morandi Museum

Cream, taupe, terne, green,
cylindrical, squat, square –
are they ideas in mufti,
these calm families crowding in
to the coveted centre?
Silence incarnate,
emptiness replete?

They reflect on us passing through
the echoing room
or standing a moment
in twos and threes and fours –
tall, short, dumpy, thin,
brown coat, beige dress, grey suit –
as we mirror them.

They are not
clumped fungi,
Fez at dawn,
gulls on a quay,
not quarterly tables of profit and loss
nor stone bouquets
for a silent order of nuns.

These infernally lovable bottles and jars
are players in a waiting game:
they see through us
an afterlife of art,
white on white, unsigned, unframed,
pure presence
migrating to light.

The Kashan

for Tina and Paul Kane

I saw it years ago.
Known at a glance,
it was like insight,
a keyhole to heaven:
framed skies of endless fall
brimmed azure, violet, indigo –
contracts from other worlds
whose terms I breathed
like incense trails
or a pattern of thought
to get by heart.
Its two dimensions
turned me drunk with blue –
I was no more
than the Kashan's waking site,
just slippage in and out
of length and breadth.
I found myself
and asked the price:
wishful thinking from Persia
at 400 knots to the inch.
So now it's memory –
a 10 by 15
target for words
whose pinpricks into 4D
make flatlander stars.
But memory's the bargain of the bazaar.
It's stuck perception –
a slick of past
for which you thumbprint then,
both cost, both gain.
The commerce between is quick
as the shimmering sex of light

or how we pulse from particle to wave,
short-changing be with have,
ghostly offspring of chance
and a small star patch.
Faster and faster now,
going nowhere I know,
I've a rug's blue map for the trip,
and habit's recurring dream:
hurriedly packing
love and sadness and shame
into the family's one suitcase,
this quantum of time.

The Korin Print

of cranes he gave
  chose its moment and fell:
a shatter of glass,

  ten stoical birds and
    a thousand perfect edges
  for weapons and jewels:

a spill of love threats,
  enchanted ice with no way back.
I'd take a stab at words like that:

  sliver-thin glints,
    shards in the sisal mat –
  my dictionary runs from alpha to chaos:

these sudden triangles
  underfoot, underhand.
The smallest flake or syllable

  may draw blood –
    the ruby on my ring finger
  is signalling stop.

The cranes stride on,
  affronting eternity in their buckled frame.
They are looking for frogs.

from *One Hundred Famous Views of Edo*
after Ando Hiroshige

The Torinomachi Pilgrimage in the Asakusa Rice Paddies

Sunset always makes her think of blood.
The shoji, blankly portioned out,
is a treaty pushed aside to seize the view.

Through the window's fine crossbars and struts,
the pilgrimage is a black ant trail in coldest light,
all shadows barred. White Fuji cannot frown.

She and her just-departed guest are guessed
behind the black silk screen through innuendos:
tissues on the floor, *kumade* pins to deck her hair.

A cloth and bowl wait on the sill by the cat,
a scruff-tailed, taut white knot in his winter fur.
He is the Overseer of the Seven Gods of Happiness

brandished above the procession crossing the marsh,
with one eye on the mice in the thatch below.
Rice straw makes his mistress think of gold,

then something left from autumn – tones and moods
which stay beyond the law, having no form or edge.
Three lines of wings departing late across

the leached-out sky, blessedly out of reach,
will erase themselves through dusk's code in the round,
but cat sits tight above the painted Yoshiwara sparrows.

The woman, lazily stretched out naked as non-
existence behind the screen, yawns and fingers a pin
whose tip's too sharp, thinks of a former friend
and a certain point to settle. One breath after

another is pacifying the room. Sunset is the gentlest
despair. Ah! she's made her thumb bleed now.

Tsukudajima Island from the Eitabashi Bridge

We must be in a boat below the bridge,
with the island just a distant squat of huts.
Sly, the way this master backflips promise,
juggles distance, makes us bridge the gap.
Beneath the high pale piers the tide slip-slops
a bickering lullaby barge-side and seaward
where a congregation rides at anchor,
and jutting from the prows of fishing boats
hung braziers send up eely tails of smoke,
sinister calligraphs like warnings
of the false round gleam below.
Though still the *shirauo* come teeming in,
tiny see-through snips of trust,
to full moon viewing time:
the instinct trap.
The fish-shaped scoop far overhead
and the ranged contagion of pallid stars
can only float a faint light down
as countersign to these transparencies
whose fate is to be rendered milky white
as the porcelain at the Shogun's court.

The Chiyogaike Pond at Meguro

In five neat leaps the waterfall is down
to the pond in which O-Chyo chose to drown.

Just here, where they once knelt, an ivory pin
slipped her hair, a minnow into the green,

and their reflections merged a moment before
he left, as men do, for some distant war.

The mist's hieratic and will only write
gnomic texts of pink and gold and white.

Tomorrow leans as blankly over their past
(seeking out some cause, just or unjust)

as these trees blossoming like lovers' vows.
The water mirrors only naked boughs.

New Year's Eve Foxfires at the Changing Tree, Oji

The beautiful is always bizarre, said Baudelaire.
Maybe the bizarre is truth at its most acute
dying away. Is all art funerary then?

Indigo's pinpricks of light, these winter stars,
ripen with night in the iron-tree.
Such pallid fires cross the waste,
and the vixen already waiting raise a paw
as if to be kissed to another life.

I remember the sultry pelt round my mother's throat,
the clack of dangling paws on her small high breasts,
the creature's canny nose, far-seeing amber eyes,
and how it became her,
all furry shoulders, scarlet nails and stalking heels.

Her scent, Ma Griffe with its cypress edge of 'if',
draws me over this marsh to a past of wavering lights –
fox fire and star, asides of thought –
till the only spoor, this trace we were,
fades out to a hunger unutterable at last.

White Event

Who bought the ivory netsuke I thought
so dear? Woman in Bath Playing with Cat.
She was leaning forward, her hair looped up with combs,
and smiling, with a dancer's open arms,

her fingers' white arpeggios stepping out
to tap the upraised paw of the little cat
full stretch on hind legs on the tub's flat rim
in a Melbourne antique shop's side room

slanting dusty sun. The owner's face
lifted. Unscrewing the cherry-wood base
of the bath, he turned it reverently to show
her secret swirls and folds, a lover's-eye view

in finest detail, slightly opened out
like the pre-germination of a tiny nut:
the woman, like the cat, rounded, complete.
I should have pawned commonsense and paid outright

to learn by lip and tongue tip like a child
the implicate order of that closed world:
the curves and crannies, the fingers tippling air
forever taunting Master Velvet Claw.

They were a dance still to the music of breath
held a short time, on another path.

Optometrists on O'Connell

The hospitality of absence:
near-abstractions facing off
in a small philosophy shop
with speculation on sale and a cut-price special
on truth – which here comes down to
a hundred vacant points of view
multiplied mercilessly in mirrors,
two plastic chairs, opaque,
and three colour magazines,
token reality nodes to slow down light.

I'm the final cause
of this purposeful unmanned eyewear
with the latest titanium frames
in queues, phalanxes, echelons, ranks,
glass behind glass behind glass.
It's a front for the murky inner room
where I sat last week fixating on
the eye of the other,
Inspector of retinas and aqueous humour,
then failed line five of his nonsense chart.

Today flame-haired Penelope
advances formally, as with Japanese tea,
bearing the rose-rimmed opticals like a crown
and lowers them onto their three-point site,
releases, stands back, breathes.
Eye to spectacled eye it's visual vertigo,
free fall into Penelope's sea-green pupils,
follicles, freckles and pores.
A slight adjustment of wings
and I'm back to the suddenly fractal street
breathing the five o'clock light,
borne on by surreal colour and shimmering form,

by paint flakes, fast food, lip gloss, tattoos, cars,
brimming windows, pockets of bright, the leaf-edge
serrations and dancing seams of the world
through the almost visible traffic noise
in the gently rising night.

Samovar

My leftover samovar thinks it is an heirloom,
connoisseur of dust, and chaperon of 1901.
Silvoed with a velvety cloth
to a grey plague gleam,
its empty belly smells of several nowheres.

This mottled shape of Britannia metal
has sussed me out with its balding silver spout
and fancy handle; teetering on its curlicue stand,
the battered traveller's journeyed twice to the Salvos,
once to the dump, and come back.

You are plainly a durable marriage
of body and soul. I couch her round warm
confirmation: *Gravity and levity*
both embrace mass.
This is our ongoing dialogue game.

The way a solar cell drinks in the sun,
these servants store us up
as playback love. Yet cannot quite be.
Except – this slight metallic pang,
an aftertaste with no true name.

Ciao, Anna Mezzanotte, at your *tavola grande*
with your *teiera inesauribile,*
what is this, anyway, pouring in and out?
Life at the lid, time at the spout –
non-attachment with a tannin grip.

Glissez, glissez, you must glide,
said Madame de Sévigné (over a demi-tasse)
and wrote it down. Any such delicate letter contains
the Last Will and Testament of Tea.
We glide away on disappearance itself –

and back – through these inheritors marking time.
I'm writing this at a café table, teapotless.
A woman at the window
is reading to her man: 'In the still of the night
they were found still playing their fiddles for joy'.

Ah, that was the Golden Age of Samovar!

Blue Bowl

This pedestal bowl against the light
shows a leftward tilt,
a yen toward some philosophy
other than fruit.
The obtuse angle makes me think
of a certain man:
what that cocked head had on its mind
was Kierkegaard not Zen.
I admire asymmetry luckily
but balance too.
So did my doctor when we were young,
lowering his stethoscope
with a little frown
then deftly tilting my left nipple back
to match its mate.
A purely aesthetic gesture
like my picking lint off his coat.
I remember we used to laugh a lot
at next to nothing.
Later I heard his marriage fell apart
and thought of that year
when we both felt
regular check-ups advisable.
Was it training or natural bent
that helped him keep things straight?

Hobart Time

Night: black mass of silence.
Into sleep's slippage
my landlady's heirloom, 1860s French,
has tethered a ghost:
the whispering tread and swish
of a taffetta ancestor, great-great-great...
paces the room with lies against death
to soothe a frightened child.

Morning: first snow on the Mount.
The Town Hall clock chimes six,
rippling air to water, coming, going,
coming, going. The iron sound
sighs through the port, dreaming direction
after the icebreaker grinding south
where night is day
and all the hours are white.

Afternoon: the deaf-mute round the bone
that watches me and tells my pulse
and needs no winding on
shines up its simple face
already haloed gold
in trust there'll be a heaven for little clocks
where time will burst its round
and dance and dance.

Evening: a dogged barking streets away,
the lonely monotone of distance.
Somewhere near at hand
(I open a window and lean out)
a little piece by Brahms
is lifting free of the nagging metronome.
Behind each earnest note
I sense the careful breathing of a child,
her steady heart.

The Arrival

after the watercolour by Thornton Walker

We are a squat of guavas
arranged to advantage on blue
or plopped in Malacca bowls
(it's a tight squeeze).
'Jade, emerald, malachite, vert,'
we murmur together,
'loden, reseda, celadon, sage' –
our gently differing opinions are always green.
From imminence to immanence
we have come –
having made the long trip
from fruit to art,
we have entered guava heaven.
Evolution was a heavy scene
and we do not intend to budge again.
From our vantage point
we watch the colour of time,
we loll,
comatose as the thighs
of the lumpy old woman of Bukit Bintang
who fell asleep in a Reject Shop
and was sold for a song.
Aeons and aeons it's been,
from primordial jelly
to a verdigris thought,
and we are exhausted, worn out, done,
utterly, utterly guava.

Carp with Suckerfish

The pond carp shine
in the sunlight, milling for
place, a goggle-eyed gulping hydra,
a slippery plait of smooth-muscled
fishness, bronze, vermilion, white and
one pure silver philosopher nosing
a stone, sensing an end to flow. Fifty
at least, pearled, mottled, plain, and
the leader, nacreous persimmon gold.
They are lovely as girls in long robes
late for school or neat-capped boys
in a pushy queue… with a thwack,
one tries to leap and fails. These are
the surface dwellers, the extroverts.
Below, hugging their shadows onto
the depths the suckerfish lie: crisp
paper silhouettes, they score them
selves out side-on, then flap and
slide and settle again – drainers
of dregs, drab makers of clarity
still as black kites stretched taut
or velvet cut and laid out: the
waistcoats of child-size mourn-
ing suits. They are Escher fish,
Fibonacci fish, shaped and
spaced by the golden mean
to an avant-garde poster for
yesterday's wall. I think of
the dark distinctions that keep
us sane, trailing my hand in
the pool. The carp with a
leisurely turn touch
and glance off
my skin

Eating Durian with Chandra

Chow Kit, Kuala Lumpur

We stopped round midnight at a hawker's stall
of durian mobiles and braided mangosteen
– haute coiffure with minibombs
– dangling echidnas in army green.

The Chinese vendor aimed his cleaver twice
Thunk! then wrenched the splits apart
Uh! on a smell as powerful as the hide
and we sat at his rickety table and ate

on the slope in the haze with one foot over the kerb,
discussing relative merits: in short, the taste's
like garlic custard in a urinal. Ah,
but more... This was the Month of the Hungry Ghosts

and the glutted shrines. I saw only a rat
patrolling a ledge in search of a window gap
as we breathed and became pure durian,
the loose flesh melting eerily ripe

as ectoplasm in August, or creamy sex
on the cunning tongue. Taboo, almost,
the pungent, savoury-sweet ambivalence
haunted our breath for hours like a sated ghost.

Giants

The cempedaks dangle like killer
jokes by Damocles,
solitary ontological puzzles,
or well-hung pairs –
prickly dichotomies weighing in:
imagine Descartes scratching his balls,
Archimedes scrambling out of the bath,
or Newton under a cempedak tree –
Salve gravitas.
If form follows function,
they're committee fruit
by Krupp and Disney and Bosch.
They hang in a private dark
in the orchard here –
Jesmi has dressed them out
in *The Star* and the *New Straits Times*:
an ageing transvestite sect
with a doomsday pact.
Their tutus yellow and droop.
Puteh slips her hand up under and feels
there were giants in those days
then bears one in like military spoils.

Limes

Limau, the Malay word, open as the snarl
of the civet cat Tamby and Daisy caught
by the shed, echoes the taste effect,
its circle of sharp surprise. Limes
themselves, dark green and tough,
seem missiles more than fruit,
neat ammo for a catapult or a children's fight,
with a taste somewhere between
austerity and assault.

Here, eating and drinking is the national sport,
and lime juice, over-sweetened and dilute,
comes with rings of ice to swivel on straws;
you spit the pips for a family game
or pitch a fallen lime at the dogs and miss.

Then remember the news report –
but that was in another country,
cancel, delete, forget the sight –
jutting out of the sand, two terrified heads,
their brief, unbearable wait
to be pelted by righteous men
for the sin of touch.

If your son and daughter ask for bread
will you give them a stone?
Yes. Time and again.

What's to be done with a handful of bitter limes?
Here – catch.

The Pangolins
for Mulaika

Throwing the I Ching by the northern wall
(Mountain over Water: the cataract clears),
rereading the dubious message in dubious light,
dusk there is as brief as thirty years.

The dogs were off at the end of the garden, barking
at moonlight or monkeys, tenor and alto and bass.
Under the rambutans it was lighting-up time,
teetering lanterns in the bushes and grass

were practising emerald – *becoming, yes, here;*
the fireflies above were loopy with desire.
A pounding of fists south-east from the Surau
was the kampong boys on their Thursday drums. The air

yearned after the odd missed beat like a tired heart.
And then the stranger came. Out of the neat
fit of the dark. Self stood back. No Name
trundled up, snuffling the mulch with her slender snout.

She was the presence of many grandmothers, homely,
buttressing wonder, nosing around the boles
of the clumped bananas, tip to tapering tip,
a relaxed bell curve validated with scales

perfectly graded – 3:5:8:13...
Her back was firm terrain under my hand,
an equable riddle with a waddle (Earth over Earth:
a friend will be lost, a friend will be found).

I squatted down. She paused and quirked her head;
this was no tree. *To run or not to run?*
To amble. With dignified haste like the shopping-bag rush
for the 5 p.m. to Rawang in Ramadan.

What goes on four legs at night and none at noon?
At dawn alert next day Suwanti chained
the dogs away from their round jungle-green enigma
then bowled the baby into the hedge to its kind.

Down Jonker Street

the antique shops are glittering dens
where dragons bare their teeth to corner gloom,
sepia maps and star charts haze the air,

and blue and white porcelain bowls
colonise teak sideboards like family
whose six generations here cradle each other

up to their ghosts in the watercolour above –
the same Malacca bowls as offerings:
seven scoops of space on fresh-laid shadow,

each rim conjured with a stroke of white –
a sliver of light between solid and void,
that pure depth with no foothold

like the quiet hour when you first learnt
to carry the dark of yourself
like a heart in your cupped hands.

I choose an ink wash painting on rice paper,
mostly see-through space
around a glaring, fiercely eyebrowed sage.

Crossing the Mekong
for Michael

Luang Prabang:
the boat was already waiting by the bank
near the women kneading their washing on the stones
when we took the cab, four planes, the bus, the tuk-tuk
and the last few steps down the dusty lane
to our unsteady seats with the boatman
pushing off sleekly to the island,
the last, we thought, in a nest of trips, with only
flimsy tickets and pocketless memory to mark the way back.
On the other side,
the reeds lacked all intention, bent to straw.
The mud-flat sucked our feet and spat out frogs
tiny and naked as embryo truths,
as if the mouths of silt could spew out light.
Through the open arches of Wat Long Khoun:
the swish of a brush broom regular as a mantra,
drifts of bougainvillea leaves and flowers,
a ripple of saffron robes across the court.
We took the narrowing path to the cave
heavy with incense, black with soot,
home to families of Buddhas squat as frogs
but not quite perfectly still –
the corners of each half smile
cast shadow thoughts,
faint notions
wavering up with the sandalwood and musk.
So this was the last stage, tracking down into the earth,
dim-lit, ordinary, a little cramped,
then back in time
for the waiting boat.

The Wardrobe

It was glossy black, lightweight, plain,
woven and framed in a clear mood
from canes gathered in by village girls
a half-day's lurching ride from a town
three borders away. It caught at dusk
the last lick of the sun
as if remembering the fretwork gold
of northern temples, arks of dream
high in the blue-smoke air.
Was it a trick of light or sleight of thought
that summoned up the honey rattan's
deeper being beneath the paint?
Back of the black wardrobe
with its coffin-shaped drawer
was a high white wall with a gap
where the bats flew in, untidy with life,
to hang their rags from a beam.
Squarely below, it stood as firm
as its own first principle, emptiness,
the space where nothing is. Where
memory equals mass at the speed of thought,
filtering through with the orchard light,
the gossip of leaves and birds,
the azan far-off and the silence between.
There was the shrill of Raslan's boys,
the whine of his power saw.
There was the ceiling fan's low hum,
the little click as I shut the door.

Travelling Towards the Evidence

We start with nothing
but darkness older than bone

and a couple of leftover maps,
some purpose lighting us down
the way a muslin curtain sifts a green day,
or a moth on your hand

makes the moment's longest lover, lifting off.
Down onto loose sand
where another man's creed
may be your grit in the craw,

or glimpsiest chiffons of God
bankrupting the one you were.
Neptune sextile Pluto sets its seed
as prayer's cross-section –

a star-fruit, say, or the pomegranate's
packed congregation.
A flower will open on sheer fall,
says Anna Mezzanotte, ironing lace.

We travel towards such evidence
trace by trace,
backwards, with our luggage
of lessening light

and wonder, our greatest gift,
prodigally rationed out –
the practised pilgrimage is
fashion's cul-de-sac.

Though Shih Tsung says the arrow
that misses the mark
also completes the aim.
Easy as gnats dance scraps of sun,

adds Anna, stretching the lace.
But don't look down,
the chasm wears a certain smile.
And some would choose

a plangent depth to joy's meniscus,
since wind will only house
a lake to the next parched grief
and jealousy will smash

a fugue apart to seize thin air
and hate you more. The cache
of memory fuels ongoing best.
While the gift of space

gentles every bend as
ambled cowbells splice
exile to a pattern of will.
The date palms of our bracketed span

may seed oases far from these dystopias
whose lost yesmen
have set their anti-hopes like mugs
on tomorrow's blackened sill.

Our cells signed on for a better deal,
body's lust for soul,
soul's for incarnation,
pain as the edge of light or the touch

of never. But the broken is
often eerily calm, and the itch
of worry scratches a lonely grave.
Look – two kingfishers,

there in the camphor laurel.
And the scent of freesias.
Fireflies. Monsoon rain.
This fern, this rock,

apple gums over a creek...
An orange flock
of butterflies once lit on my head;
two deer at dawn

stretched their necks timidly polite
and stared me down
with weapons of trust.
Cynicism's copper and lime

is a coin on the tongue
for Charon's deep pockets; time
as a brief ID is the happiest fake.
What god of the unlikely gets us here?

With Pepe and Isabelle, say,
and the saturnine stare
of twelve cooked goat heads
watching us sip goat broth

in Jemaa el-Fna;
how friends of a day can enter your breath.
Under the clock
in an empty Metro late at night

we were reading *The Rights of Man*
when the lights went out.
Smiling in Turkish, joking in Arak,
laughing in Greek,

you mix the words for want
and love and like;
all journeys nest like Russian dolls
or strike footloose

through no man's land;
daring's a pilgrim flapping an empty purse.
We bartered and bargained,
held horizons in doubt,

held the other a gain,
bypassed small nightmare states
forbidding dreams,
lost one cause after another,

harvesting stars in a mist
or cancelled out by a weather
of beauty that whorled
camellia petals beyond our art

to a pattern of fall. We pushed the mirage
too far; the dragon kite
battled the wind to a joint defeat.
Now my route,

redrawn, files by the
Gustavian burial vault's
plain pewter parcels,
patient lost property waiting in line –

en namnlös dotter död vid födseln
says the smallest one:
a daughter, nameless, dead at birth,
1621.

In the train, two deaf-mute boys
were turning thought to sign
with hands like courting birds
riding an easy wind.

Such lovely behaviour of eyebrows,
such shrugging goodbye at Lind!
Where powerlines like blind lepers
led on through a Brueghel frame.

But I'm no guide, I've camped in swamps
and forgotten my name
a hundred ways. No one, Ulysses knows,
compels us to steer by the moon.

And love? A clinical care
does more in a yellow fever zone.
Je suis un cimetière abhorré de la lune.
That crosses the mind, alone,

and will not die.
Like the narrow pass to Petra's rose-red stone,
or a fallen aloe flower
pointing the way to a hidden spring.

Listen: the chuckling of underground water,
the crickets' glossy song
after the long day's drums.
Twilight's candle power is the zeal

of the hunchbacked woman in San Giovanni
clearing the fall
of tallow, straightening the tapers.
Madonna, the vastness of that space

where everything's possible for someone else.
You can sing it as praise,
but the anti-lyric works miracles too;
even belief

must wear the cloak of another's doubt.
To advance with a knife
against the aajej
cuts short the miles to Babylon. Now home

is an arid word with too much coast,
boat people left to the storm
or lost in emptiness,
this Martian state of saltbush, scattered bones,

red earth, and fly-latched lips –
Laconia's place of stones.
Small faces range behind barbed wire
like tinsel strung

for a stillborn Christ. Children unstitch our lips,
Slug-in-a-Sac so longs
for a safe place this side of turbulence.
Slug has turned dumb

at racks of bodies left on public view,
the school made death museum.
What words could serve as guides
for a starless hour?

No obsequious abstracts. See!
The Leonids – summer's meteor shower –
lions salient, from *salire* leap.
The elliptical travelling-on.

You think you can improve the world?
I do not think it can be done.
The ones we were arrived in Port-au-Prince
singing of profit and loss –

such odd songs tack together
our torn race.
The square black sail swells out,
the small white boat

skims over the usual waves
with its hopeful loot.

The Cut

Yesterday, killing time
in a draughty booth with Signorina Domani,
I could hear the rickety sideshows
touting their sinister glitz
while the old hands dexterously fixed to go
with screeches and cries like guy ropes
sheeting out August sky,
the big top already an open shroud
on the trampled grass.

What's to become of us, Signorina,
the whole caboodle forever shunted on?
I cut. She dealt them orderly out: ten,
face down like a cyclone in disgrace.
Leaning in to the moment,
her white face was a slammed door.
I remember her breath sucked in,
her hand abruptly turning up
the Hanged Man and the Five of Cups,
a slight hesitation over the Nine of Swords,
and never a word.

If I had reached out then
and stroked that pallid cheek,
citing the softest law of physics,
the purest equations of song,
would I have felt the trembling of the pack,
would I have heard?
But I was young and sure that time
had solid walls. Bright house of cards!
The least thing salvaged long enough
turns treasure though –
a sagging sequin on her cloak

pooling the glow of the lamp.
Somewhere outside
a child laughed sharply in surprise,
first tasting the soft grey light.

Heirlooms

with a line from Philip Levine

Spite's needle, spleen's black junket, crystal's ice,
a pitted thimble, voodoo masks, a voice
on tape, with fault lines faltering into blame

like the shadow of sheet lightning striking home.
The jars of jam along the pantry shelves
glowed in the safe half-dark like unlived lives;

silverfish hid in the widening cracks of walls
and under the wallpaper's lifting yellow curls.
The old house smelled of tin and soap, the sad

stale breath of female feuds, of string and lard.
Twilight colonised the cellar steps
by noon as cutting words and tightened lips

slicked the scissors slung on its kitchen hook.
The ravenous silver of that open beak
where 'should' and 'will' met along one plane

would gulp its own fierce thirst as the sentenced man
aching for water feels his throat clamp shut,
spilling the priceless stream to left and right.

Family was a wandering divide
with potlatch grudges hoarded either side.
And we would play a game of Blind Man's Bluff,

undercover agents feeling for laughs,
follow the whispered footsteps, brush an arm,
graze the wainscot, stumble against a jamb,

smashing at last Grandmother's treasured urn
whose scattered porcelain crumbs were feasts of pain.
But darkness codes the light – snaps in a drawer:

the ninetieth birthday party, what was the year?
Twenty champagne glasses, shoulder height,
with one white face breaking the circle of light,

my brother looking back across the room
to where thrift kept the corners rich with gloom.
To when our eyes would meet beyond the game

of I Spy, Pass the Parcel, Hide the Harm
of passing time with rumour it was tame.
They feed they Lion and he comes. He comes.

For time was spending us with none to spare
loved enemies who made us what we were.
Writing into the night, I feel the words

sliding away to silence on both sides,
thankless promissory notes come late.
With each heartbeat, they'd say, you pay the debt.

The Summerhouse

Some strange wind had wafted it from afar
to roost between the orchard and the vines;
its latticework made lozenges of air
and shadowy Chinese chequers over the stones.

North and east and west were welcomed in
at three low arches; down the south end the light
was split apart and splashed across your skin
deep cordials and elixirs, jelly-bright.

Red, yellow, green, and furthest blue,
the stained-glass panes were finely etched
with leaves and buds. You could see through
to other worlds and almost reached

golden Arabia and burning Mars,
a thrice-enchanted wood of emerald green,
and a violet country, deep and mysterious,
calling you to remember and return.

But on the very hottest days,
the leather sofa was the coolest place:
we reached down Grimm's from Grandpa's glass bookcase,
for Hans, Snow White, Falada, Briar Rose,

slain children, witches, wolves, and hacked-off toes.
Tingling, we turned a page. The empty house
breathed and waited; we sensed the slightest noise
and thought of the sun, the green and welcoming trees.

'More haste, less speed!' called Gran. Pell-mell we raced
along the dark hall rounding in on us
and into the blazing light to press up close
to the summerhouse's safe blue paradise.

Dividend

Saturday, late morning, the fever began:
the short phone calls to the little man
that Aunty Bubbles knew, the form and weight
and starting price. 'They're lined up at the gate
for the fourth at Victoria Park.' The nasal voice
of the wireless galloped us fast as the winning horse.
'It's Valiant Boy by a short half-head.'
'Oh pooh,' our mother said, 'another dud.'

But when she wore her lucky hat to the races
once, her Uncle Clarry's grey, Sir Croesus,
came home on the rails at fifty to one.
He gave a pound note each to me and John,
and a taste for risk; we learned to back long shots,
dark horses, elderly relatives, and red hats.

Brownhill Creek

After the miles of dusty road, the shade
was another season of willow, moss, dogwood.
The blackberry-hidden creek and its creatures called.

A sunning stone on a stone pulsed at the throat.
We tried the grey-green water tasting of slate,
soft rot and stillness; the morning sifted light

through fennel weed and showed where yabbies hid;
flies flicked at the shining skin and on each side
the fat black taddies queued to suck the mud

which pushed its silk between our toes and made
small clouds. Topaz eyes watched from the reeds;
John slipped and splashed but caught the frog – pure white,

he danced in the jar on the one back leg he had
and when we tipped him out he kicked off hard.

Wings

With two umbrellas from the chicken yard,
in our mother's cape from the trellis top
trailing wisteria, from the roof of the shed
with a parasheet and a Doppler cry, we'd leap

into pansies and phlox, love-in-a-mist
and soft turned earth. Something buoyed us up
each time to jump again, trembling and bruised.
Weight was not countered by a longer drop.

We changed our tack one Sunday of high wind,
blew up our thirty-seven saved balloons
and ran light-headed, yelling, behind
red, blue, yellow, buffeting pink, white, green,

with Roger barking up and down the lawn
and failed to fly. And never tried again.

History Lessons

Between the fretwork strips of the walnut wireless
semi-tuned through static to the Early News
came the BBC tones of the ABC.
Next to Nipper the foxie,
one ear cocked to His Master's Voice,
my own ear flat to the console's
stretched cloth cosy with dust
and a faint singed smell like history lessons,
I heard the name
(knees to my chin just then I saw
blood spots, the first, on my pink pajamas),
and raced to my parents' bedroom with the news,
'Stalin is dead! Joseph Stalin is dead!'
My mother hushed me to the bathroom,
trussed me up with safety pins and a pad
then turned the wireless up and left it on all day
like a coffin over and over declaring its corpse.
My father couldn't stop smiling,
'Well, young lady!' and, to my mother,
'Beria probably bumped him off.'
Someone was dead
and we were allowed to be glad.
All day some distant darkness spilled through me...

Drawing Mermaids

It was him from across the road.
Leaning over her shoulder.
'Is it a mullet or a trout?'
She linked the scales like choppy seas.
'You've drawn the breasts too low.'
He was making her mad.
'Come over home
and I'll show you in my Gray's.'
She finished the chainmail silently but went.
He spread some paper on his desk
and traced her outline gently as he drew.
It prickled her breath.
'The nipples here, about the fourth rib level.
And now the belly button – ping!'
It wasn't a mermaid, it was a girl.
He coloured her dark between the legs.
That prickling feeling again,
'You've done the feet all wrong.
Besides, she's fat.' Something
was making her very cross.
He stood up, 'Alright, fierce Miss Flounce,
let's finish off the cake.'
When she got home
she took her clothes off in the front bedroom
and looked in the scalloped glass:
two points, anemone pink,
and a seaweed patch.
She didn't mind it after all.
Besides, *she* wasn't fat.
She stroked it softly as a small stray cat.

The Egyptian Room
South Australian Museum

Stillness rose from the stone and wood
and earthenware: they breathed in mysteries
lightly, carefully touching all they could –
the hunting mural, Khafra's cold black knees.

Here was lapis lazuli, a scarab race,
green figurines of Hathor, Bast and Thoth,
hungry for souls, the jackal Anubis
and the mummy of a cat in stained brown cloth.

The moon by night, the sun by day –
blue Horus eyes to ward off harm
gazed up at them. The Lady Tiy
smiled from her corner, knowing, calm.

Still bright on the cedar coffin's lid
was the Twenty-seventh Dynasty face
of Renpit Nefert. 'There's really nothing inside.'
They rattled the locked door of the case.

'I bet there is!' 'Bet there's not.
Anyway, I'm going to see the hive.'
They smelt the honey, furry-body sweet,
in the steady hum of being alive.

The sun was high. *I am Khepera at dawn*
Ra at noon and Tum at eventide.
They and the lotus column on the lawn
cast no shadows on the world outside.

Ice-Oh!

Although we loved the gentle horse whose nose
of worn-out velvet nudged us for ryegrass,
Antarctica come to the suburbs was what drew
us through the heat; we trotted by its slow
and straining bulk or swung on the creaking cart.
Only the iceman galloped – through each gate,
bent double over the hessian-covered block
that weighed him down the side, around the back
and in with never a knock, boots puddling mud
over lino, to clunk on the chest edge, teeter and thud.
Hot-foot, hot-foot, on the road we'd wait,
breathing the wet sack smell, the oats, the sweet-
sour yellow dung, force-feeding weeds to Horse
to earn our chunks of slithery dripping ice.
'Now clear off kids – and mind the bleedin' wheels.'
So perched on the fence we kicked our heels,
watching the cart lurch up to Duthy Street.
Johnny always waved as it turned right
and into just a faint clip-clop applause;
while fast as we could suck or slurp, our ice
was licked off at the corners by the sun
or sent in shivery runnels down our skin,
trickling chocolate drops across the dirt.
And when we held the chips up glistening bright,
greyly among the frozen bubble swarms
there went a crooked mile between the palms
to question-mark the light. Beyond us, time
hung round on the wall; at every touch was home –
green streets, my brother's laugh, a sunny day,
only half-grasped, forever melting away.

Climbing the Nectarine Tree at Dusk

The tree is growing upward fast, greedy for light,
with the best fruit already out of reach.
She wedges one bare foot where the branches fork
then steps up into the sway of boughs.
The young tree takes her weight.
Between the fingering leaves
yesterday's stars just meeting her sight
are cold fire fruit hurtling out and away –
no fixed object in the universe.
It could be a practice one, she thinks,
a training ground for light and dark got out of hand
with earth the kindergarten of kiss and kill
(stubbornly trying to think the pattern deeper,
filling her aproned shirt, starting back down).
She sits in the cool deep clover thinking
whatever. Looking up into December. Being rich.
Then spreads the nectarines out, splits one,
sinks in. Summer syrups down her chin.
The quietness ripens into silence then ripens back.
She tries to tell scent-taste apart. The tongue can't,
nor the mind trying the flavour of thought,
mixing sense and image and word:
a secret smile with a faintly bitter curve?
Or being fourteen with new breasts,
whispering 'sin'?
Another soft bite, slurping the luscious flesh.
Just 'nectarine'.
That tree knows what it's doing.
And there's Sirius out now. Seeming
to hold steady.

Zachary and the Angel

When Zachary came to stay and
smashed the terracotta angel on a stone
and ran and hid, being only three,
my grandmother opened her eyes again
and smiled and drew me back through years of sun
as though to brush my hair, outside on the lawn.
Zachary pressed, breath held, against a wall,
his *What if?* gone to bits –
hands and wings strewn under the birdbath
cupped to heaven were evidence and warning
'So' would soon descend.

My grandmother set the hairbrush on the grass,
Don't get in such a tizz!
patiently teasing out a knot
as my heart went yes no yes
(I'd broken a second-best plate)
in time with small wild Zachary poised for flight,
his face like sunlight blotted out.
Off you go and play, drawing my blonde hairs
out of the brush, *I'll fix that blessed plate*.
Least said, soonest mended.

When Zachary fell asleep
I mixed the Araldite claggy
and eased the first wing back:
a swimming together, a tiny abrasion
then instant rapport, the intimate pleasure
of matchmaking an almost perfect fit,
or patching a quarrel up, head, hand and heart.
The cracks shone pinkly as proud flesh.

And the darker path of repair that
zigzagged over the willow-pattern bridge

would be the very strongest part
my grandmother said with a serious nod.
Next day, Zachary's wide-eyed start –
the cherub, miraculously intact,
perched back on the rim of the bowl.
He watched and watched the juggle of wrens
turn water to light.

The Trellis Fence

being a heavy investor in space
            is half inclined to flight
so I've hedged its bets
            threading the tipply bougainvillea through
to the neighbour's side and back
            greening this graph of chance
its vertical why and horizontal how
            so the sinuous branches surge
diagonal as a stellar run on the Footsie or the ASX
            with one long overarching bough
dipping yes and swaying no
            searching some further purchase for upside
(my winter peach tree, say)
            and meeting wind
as a question mark in flower –
            magenta bunchlets, glossy hooks, pale buds
so overleaping any trope with tropism
            I've left intention to its own co-ordinates.
The damp half-naked backyard
            intimates thought, the cool bare
abstracts angle in. I'll have to prune them back
            the vine and tree, a sort of tiny, necessary pain –
dark energy tied to matter hurls us on.
            They say the universe forgets itself
and starts again. One way-out speculator says
            that disappearance-ripples enter each new time
so nothing of love and green will travel on
            as profit but the edge of loss.
Maybe we need another part of speech –
            little time words,
presuppositions to twine our concepts
            through, then back, higher-dimensioned with now.
In flower. Holding on. Ungeared with doubt.
            Listen – the gentle old arthritic drawl of chooks
the soft concurrence of doves on the fence
            half-knowing why all this should ever be.

Winter Solstice

At the teetering of the year,
a small girl's hopping a half track
through the frost, left foot, left foot,
then standing astride the first long rays
and stripes of shade
as June sun fans through the
promise and proof of the snowdrop leaves.

The pergola's cast the shape of a torii
over the lawn – linked guardians
of the dynasties of gone –
the shadow of making is unforeseen.
But dance is one of the safer bets,
her body's glancing flight's
too fast for dogma's upraised foot.
The level earth she's dancing on is all horizon
flowering with leaps and cries –

the ragged tin-can orison of next door's rooster
clearing the phlegm in his scarlet throat,
flutter-tongue, double-tongue, querulous treble.
In the silence under each sole
the root tree steadies its counterpart
whose lemon-scented limbs share out the day
in scalene triangles of lightening sky.

Now fine rain's falling into this luminous place
that's leased her to its dance of fire.
See-saw, Margery Daw,
the moment's solstice is down,
she'll skip the darkness in between.
And is her play the shadow
of a bright particular being,
umbra and penumbra rimmed with light?
I read somewhere that questions in a poem
are fascist. Why?
Well winter's the quietest laughter at all that.

Freesias

Two sceptics at odds may cancel out
like minus signs to say Why doubt?

See where I've planted the Snowdon corms
between the stones. Too shallowly: the leaves
splay out, bent to a world of wind;
we tread the green flames unawares.
September will turn us – Ah! Japanese,
the air round their creamy cups spreading a covenant,
Sadness-Joy. Like wind chimes touching the edge of song,
or a small high window's mouthful of sky.
Breathe in their fragrance now,
the rush of yes but, if, maybe,

till the ghostly sacs of the lungs swell out
and airiest Other floods the brain. You too, Martin,
come back into the sun, I have picked you a percept, here –
a straggly bouquet of Being, quite unconcealed,
and it knows you, bronchiole and cell,
it is soothing the labyrinth to a safety net,
calming the rivers of blood as they leave and arrive.
Would you say it's beyond the play of beyond,
this scent – the hint of a universe drifting apart
like philosophy's fine dissolve?

Almost unbearable sweetness anyway.
Almost thought.

Honesty

Alias Lunaria: silver dollar or silver shilling,
it travels well: hold it up to the light and see

frugal savings for a rainy day.
To be honest my first reaction's the honest lie

that hopes the means will justify the end,
metaphor's sideways lean to claim a wider view

for the little everythings to hand,
these loony purses of loose change

for the futures market, translucent not transparent,
since honesty wouldn't presume on absolute truth

and isn't a fool. Lunaria means 'forgetfulness',
but all September options get snapped up.

Right now, each pod is one hand clapping the wind,
beautifully brittle, an archaeological find;

or else dry whispers tethered on wispy stems,
lesser moons resisting spin-off, interest paid to the void.

To step a little further from the truth,
they are elegant quizzing glasses, deliberately dim

like the lenses Baruch Spinoza ground
to trick his friends, blurred monocle-jokes

on one-eyed world views, even his own.
Nonsense, honesty says, I am simply the shortest distance

between two seeds. Lens or not, I magnify. Money or not,
I circulate. Give me away, I return tenfold;

rub me between your finger and thumb till I shine.
That's honesty in winter, every virtue has four seasons.

And I've told you nothing at all of the flowers in spring tra-la,
their illusory clouds of white and purple and white.

Zinnias

O fiercely classical rectitude,
brazen offerings
on puritanical stems,
rippled plates of delight
on righteous pedestals,
biblical as in the Song of Songs,
I honour you.
Red-pink-orange-creamly
formal hierarchies of lower air,
your gold dust centres
happiest pannikins.
Each day your stems persist,
small saints of ikebana,
I straighten further my spine.

They've struck a Carnivale pose:
five now fully spread
by the oval lawn
at different well-judged heights
like stepping stones to insight,
zinniaplomb appropriating Zen.
Deep pastel as the plucked
flowers of Cézanne,
each petal ripple
stoically waves goodbye
Greek-beckoning style.
Per ardua ad astra
was my father's creed.
He loved these flowers,
their poise and fortitude and edge
brightening toward the stars.

The Irises

The art of losing is a one-way trip,
the art of letting go is a return.
That blue wheelbarrow heaped with leaves
and the empty air above.
The wind chimes get the drift
then lose it again,
the way that music borrows space
to clothe the body of time.

My timber ceiling creaks in the sun;
grey cat sleeks her fur by the open door.
Stillness. Tiny leaps in the dark –
the axons' LCD of love.
Over the pinewood floor
the slats of the blind
are casting a chequer board;
you could set your pieces up
to play at win and lose
till the sun moved on to erase the game.

In the stillness after a death
you go about a room
touching a table or chair,
a vase, your face, a flower.
To be held back here in trust.

On a small low table I've set down
an empty spectacle case, open
as if a butterfly just lifted out.
There is my camera closed
on the promise of smiles,
and the square black bible from school
with its rainbow crocheted bookmark
of Celtic rings and crested snakes

gone to ground in chapter ten of Job.
The irises have opened overnight:
Fine China, offering back all light
but its opal shimmer of water,
a spiritual economics of least as most,
the ordinary, mysteriously afloat.
And there – Stygian Purple is practising night
but breathing a hint of twilight back
in courtesy to colour.

The wind chimes idle out their magpie thoughts.
The tall white iris is barely swaying now –
a small child striving to stand up straight,
the last tremblings of a tired head.

Fern

The idea of the shadow of a fern
caught in grey shale, a crosier's lean
scepticism, fingerprints on light,
have kept a century arguing half the night,

rifling the long memory of stone
whose finest thinkers filter down
from outer time's thin crust
green hypotheses of leaf and wrist.

Death's emanations they half understand –
a patterned lack of rock, absent ground,
but only the far-out theorists, sand and loam,
hold being is the horizon of time.

The molten centre seething on and on
shapes solid earth and draws it down again:
a dark relentless will to learn
the idea of the shadow of a fern.

More on the Dinosaur

No wonder they almost died out,
with one full minute between stubbed tail and ouch,
their logic couldn't connect cause and effect.
Sex was an enigma – buoyed up in the mire,
cryptogams fringing their jaws,
and their little eyes glassy with time lag,
they'd quite forget, between effort and ecstasy,
just what they were at
(the other already wallowing off).
Imagine the bliss of brontosaurs –
embracing a mountain, incurring an earthquake –
love as a natural disaster.
But the urge to survive went deep:
they're with us still, in hindbrain, basal ganglia,
sometimes a stranger's eyes, and always
man's hidden part, blunt id,
barbed as the collared head of Triceratops,
a tip on tomorrow's winner.

Flittermouse

From the eastern edge of absence
an eerieness slewed in more slant
than Emily D in Sunday black,
lobbed through a shocking slippage of air
right onto the bedside table,
a grinning foetus
between the clock and the glass,
myopically gathering in
the selvage edge of dusk
to the appliqué edge of a mask
at a gothic window over the Grand Canal,
Vivaldi, faintly, from an inner room.
The delicate, sinister skin
might have been grief's gift paper
stretched round its own dark nub which
tinily loomed, flumped towards me twice,
then upped to the edge of the Japanese print
to hang like dishevelled sci-fi,
gravity's womb,
or a scatological statement on art.
I let her be all night through chittering dreams,
but woke at dawn as she sounded space,
tracking her own grace notes to where
through the fast-thrown-open door
she took my breath away like an exorcism,
that most intimate loss.

Ech
idna
a stook
of fossil
hay spook-
ed to move
stops the ant
hole's yellow
cone, his tongue
exactly right for
the tight hole dry of
black lava he nuzzles in, ruthless,
for five or six earth-scattering seconds.
He's gone and crumbed his snout, this shoulder-sham-
bling sumo waddle on littlest legs, this small decision teeter-
ing in the balance. His charcoal spines tipped veldt grass
yellow close cosy as feathers snugging an owl, a strokable neat-
ness dappered down slick to centre back and tailed with a
cactus cowlick. At my step he's horripilous, digging in, all stop-
start as if in doubt: does hunger give him second thoughts? I touch
the fine flat central spines and feel him think, a shrinking-in like
ripples of water over stone, then further into the leaves he's gone like
a housewife in a huff frumping off early under the quilt in a warning
of curlers. I scatter bark on the last ruffed quiff. The path he's
come is a waste of snuffed ant nests and deeper holes by crumbling
logs – this patch of scrub is all echidna dreaming: the amber
fuzz of banksia, the fallen sheoak cones, the dried-out grass trees
hunkered down going to ground like this samurai loner, all
swagger, shimmy and shove, who nevertheless will need, come
spring, a whole like-minded team to trundle a channel
around his touchy mate before
the goal's up under
and in.

On the Avenue

Distinct above the traffic roar,
some pipsqueak was giving its territory away –
five glassy notes then five more
like echoes in the stripped trees' winter air,
so twig by twig by twig
the naked plane was hung with tinsel,
baubled like a boutique musical pine,

the unseen wren so much ahead of itself,
so much a sprung intention,
it seemed the tree was plucking the bird
from note to note, from now to now,
playing out flight in silver palindromes.

While passing below, our trivial quarrel
held its ground with words like
cracked bells melted down for guns
till aptly we went underground at Iéna,
parting finally at a junction
grey as a tunnel in purgatory,
no buskers at any coordinate of space or time.

Ibis

Side on – inscape's outline,
front on – a slit in the wind
riffling the yellow down beneath the grey.
As tail shucks off late rain,
his trembling makes an interface,
human/bird.
The ugly-noble beak lifts, hyperbolic –
Akhenaten's quizzical look –
swizzles the spring air momently
then left, right, left, like a blindman's stick,
dibs down for grubs.

Ibis was glyphed to science and poetry once,
a god encrypted into Luxor stone,
those crisp-edged pools
of granite shadow defying time:
I am thy writing palette, O Thoth
and I have brought unto thee thine ink-jar.

Still between two worlds, the ibis goes
scribing his way on muddy grass for worms,
kneading the earth with dreamy grace steps,
hunched as an immigrant under his luggage of light.
Each step dips his head as to the Torah or Koran.

Jutka remembers these birds
along the camp perimeters, inside and out,
near other stick-thin legs in hungry air
with flight a pallid absence.

But this is luckier terrain:
a strip of Sydney park, Elizabeth Street,
with minimal traffic fumes.
Leisurely with our sandwiches in thin sun,

we park-benchers watch each softly closing claw
lift as from a Chopin étude,
a music of silence posing as bird,
then spread out down on earth again,
millennial with resignation.

His meal is a pilgrimage to here and now:
I am everything that is the case.
The distance he gathers in,
stern and gentle as mist,
is slowly changing its mind.

This Instant

The Silver Gulls
spaced out,
hunch like poets in the doldrums,
fronting the white noise of ideas
without a peep;
a pastel wash of thought
turns froth on the grit.
Twenty red-rimmed chilly stares
wipe out the globe
as if they'd scrawled till 2 a.m.
in a critical zone,
upstaged by all that airy potential,
those hendecasyllables endlessly rolling in.
Leave us at least a sign –
wavery renga
claw-printed through marram grass,
the odd *craaark* in rant pose.
Silent, on the shore of possibly
nothing, they wait
under a sky-blue question
by equivocations of sea.

Ceiling Starlings
get the jitters.
Out on the roof till late,
they tack over emptiness
and back,
six pairs of claws
skidding apart on tin –
the Misses Left skating after the Messrs Right
for all the world
like doing eurhythmics to Philip Glass
or reading Timmy Tiptoes in cuneiform.

O 'gregarious birds of black and brown
speckled lustrous plumage',
come back in.
The OED says they're Germanic (*staraz, staron*).
Don't mention Dasein,
Being-in-the-ceiling is bad enough.
I scuffle straw thoughts in my nesting-box
till they settle down,
my live-in vermin birds
named for fledgling stars and loving rhymes.
I wish them prophetic dreams
of distant derelict sheds.
First light they are hedonists again
– PhD, Heidelberg (failed) –
screeching small joy to shreds.

Id Blinks
total eclipse of the sun
over San Lazzaro. Mini travesties
of the monks are hanging out
like black handkerchiefs in the pines.
There are nests in the silence between
the Byzantine and the surreal.
'Nevermore' is wearing away
the pentatonic scale
to sound rings like dying haloes
or shadow quoits over the pole of why.
All the plagiarists here have smoker's throat.
They tenant no fixed space,
always already evicted again,
shift the occult
to vaudeville, or stand by in the wings
like hired cloaks for a disappearing act
you can see straight through –
small sardonic souls of wayang lace,
claw raised, screen torn, last twitch.

Quo vadis, Corvus?

This Instant

the honeyeaters' cries pierce light...
the grevillea spikes are trembling
with flickers of bird
maybe, maybe,
sipping at spider-flowers
head down, grey and yellow.
Even here, gold and its shadow:
at the grass-roots level
the weeds are takeover bids;
at the end of the day
the bees choose mergers;
a butterfly floats
its banner against Monsanto,
orange and black like a dying sun
pushed up against bars.
B sharp, shriek the little birds, B sharp,
the edge of survival tastes of honey.

Listen

two ring doves hidden in green
obsessively auditing peace.

Gnats

in clouds above the river's sheen
loop in and out
the ceaseless maze they are,
being both particles of light
and waves of gnat,
thought's tiny juggling feat
and more –
the whine of a new idea
at the bright meniscus
of mind.
On such an afternoon
Heisenberg might
have come to formulate
his $\Delta x . \Delta p \geq h/4\pi$:
uncertainly, I
pin down neither gnat nor thought
but strain
at this paradigm for a poem.
Over the gnats and me
marshmallow cumulus
sail by:
far-off thought balloons,
to us,
blank as eternity.

Shifting the Dark

Not joy's aura of butterflies
nor gnats returning like pollen to the bloom.

Not the resurrection beetle
nor yesterday's ritual pavane

for a honeycomb riddled with cold –
the family myth was in the sting:

Great-granduncle set on by a swarm
tongued glistering obsidian,

a mad mosaic eclipsed the sun.
I choose the spirit-green of fireflies,

drifting afterthoughts at the river's edge,
ghost shuttles, elf breath, nimbus of limbo.

Think of a light left on past any hope of return,
oblivion underwriting desire.

Such crosslife clues for stars,
these perfect strangers do no harm;

they are heart space from the void,
round trips shifting the dark

with the simplest argument:
I shine therefore I am.

The Bees

Shamsi Tabriz by a sunny wall is watching the drunken joy of straggler bees under the marble offcut of a daylight moon. He's called up Rumi to share a scheme: a notation for truth – like music.

October brings the wild bees
back to my wooden eaves still smelling of last year's swarm.
But the crack's blocked up.
They dance their holy No, daemonic Yes,
angry as amnesia at a white hole, wanting in.
The top speed of their being, tiny gales of wings full on,
will will will find a way in, will.
A milling noise distilling down to three crammed notes
is rising and falling with the breeze.
It's a heat sound focused as the bite of honey,
fine as the sting's black thread with its dragged mouthful
of white death flesh when any ism will serve the tribe.

'The little dancing feet would ascend and descend the scale, sharp as honey, in dissonant melodies various and delicious as the stars.'
Rumi nods.

They are dying to get in –
through the ventilators into the cavity wall.
Dying in earnest to get in,
the fanatics who take the wrong turn
into my empty hive of a room.
By morning the windowsill is a hospice;
feeble, groping huddles and heaps
have burst their honey-packed bellies against the glass,
glimpsing the great god Sky.

On the wall is a Tuscan landscape framed in pine;
the pause of cypresses piercing the blue
means tenderness too late. Small body. Lost.

This one, say, curled like a waiting birth,
a striped clown child.
Down the hall the icebox hums like an arctic hive
with its one cell packed, an isolation ward.
I imagine a negative dialectic of the bee,
holding that right-hand jargon at arm's length
and closer, in my left, this nested body
as airy-light as its own flight path.

'Yes, friend Shams, truth is roundly plural, many voices, many songs. I imagine wings.'

Morning, the rest are installed and established,
that first slight honey smell, already easingly corrupt
as a quiet temptation to riches and rot.
Neither or both.
I watch the bob of their polished abdomens
inching in through the eight round holes
like backward births,
the coming and going of leisurely thoughts
turning the idea of cellar to attic.
As if id and superego were teaming up
to edge the 'I' of 'me' right out.

'Then another refractory task,' says Shams. 'I propose a glossary of light as flight to list its least divorce from the harem of here.' The beautiful spurned by the absolute, thinks Rumi – 'Are colours then the orphans of light?'

By noon, they are incessant as the sun,
the air's beset by particles fierce as time,
that nervy shudder, precipitate nectar of sound:
imagine the music of the atom,
a trembling like untolled being,
or the inside-out of love,
the ruthless edge of No Mind.

Harmonics theory is herewith colonised,
the labyrinth sings in gold.

Shams considers, 'Also our inheritance. Colour may be another clue to birth and death. We are most clearly what we give back.'

Evening is circling now,
bringing the gold grain home from salvia, daisy,
cosmos, lad's love, sage.
In the innermost confines the syrupy magma
is ceaselessly fanned, a righteous sound
like pent-up blood or war's brooding bass
rising and falling to a still fist.
A choice: to be possessed
by pale thick nothing, its wax and wane,
or acid honey's sweet overkill –
white danger, black danger? Us. Them.

'Do bees smell colour, see fragrance, perhaps?' Rumi wonders aloud, 'And could we so circle and lift, God willing, from humblest shades of umber and brown to hidden humilities of light?'

My house is throbbing with hellish heaven.
They'll have to go.
Emil from Cairo, voluble, quick, arrives
with small-business semi-assurance –
'Bees is very stubborn.'
He claims the territory with powder, spray, and filler gun –
'These lot can't be saved.'
In half an hour he's done. 'For now.' Leaving his card.

'Yes: suppose the spirit as roach or slater scurrying up to learn the bees' dance of direction. Beyond might seem no further off than this warm wall. Ah, Rumi – to see the spectrum of the dark!'

Gone, all that jitter and shove
zagging their lob flight,

keeping airborne their luggage of know-how,
a landscape of flowers fined down in the guts of the dark
to purest self.
There is an absence.
The air's still redolent of them.
But I won't think guilt. Attention is a small respect.
A temple and prison of instinct houses us too.
What manner of love is enzyme?
Tell me Jalaluddin Rumi!
What light can you cast on time, Shamsi Tabriz?

'This moment – the taste of invisible honey!' Shams Tabrizi shifts his back and sighs. Rumi narrows his eyes into blue distance.

I remember a swarm of bees spiralling once
by a leafy canal in France,
meditating, seeking something.
On the cool stone edge, I was dangling my legs,
watching the bees
and the homely little boats queued back from the lock.
Happy cargoed in sad,
as I didn't then guess.

Shingle

An earlier pitch of light
had turned all edges halo – tree, rock, child –
contained the change a moment
then withdrawn.
The pebbles banked along the cliffs
and scattered down the sand to the shore
are facing the falling day;
too many to be touched or known
except by passing air,
they sit seaward of their only gesture –
the shadow cloak cast slowly back
till the cusp of revelation,
that last delicious slice of light, goes down
into blue yesterday's digesting sound.
While the breeze, light-fingered,
dints the water's sheen to pocket
spills of early dark,
all things are making their escape
into the nether time, certitude first,
with subtleties, always in profile,
last from sight.
Listen: that other-century sound of seagull cries.
What's waiting behind all this?
Some great happiness, says Amichai.
As if they are a million doorstops
propping the unseen open a crack
the pebbles persevering from white to grey
sit put in such rapt humbledom
as the tide creeps in to round them down
in the image of their sun
(small exiled asteroids, sad moons)
that the tumbled glug and glottal stop,
the clink and crepitation,
all the blurred octaves of wind and sea

say suffer and live, suffer and live,
in pebble tongue:
opacity again and again
trying to clear to song,
always almost ahead of itself
like small feet running on hope
just gone just gone just gone...
but then... what interest has hope
ever vested in finitude?

Acknowledgements

A number of the new poems in this book were previously published in *Antipodes*, *Arc Poetry Magazine*, *Best Australian Poems 2009*, edited by Robert Adamson (Black Inc., 2009), *Best Australian Poems 2012*, edited by John Tranter (Black Inc., 2012), *Best Australian Poems 2014*, edited by Geoff Page (Black Inc., 2014), *Festschrift for Fleur* edited by Janet Wilson and Rod Edmond (New Zealand Studies Network, 2014), *Mascara*, *Perihelion*, *Prayers for a Secular World*, edited by Kevin Brophy and Jordie Albiston (Inkerman & Blunt, 2015), *Quadrant*, *Take Five*, edited by Adrian Caesar, (Shoestring Press, 2009), *The Warwick Review*, and *Wet Ink*.

I am grateful to Arts South Australia for the assistance of a Project Grant in 2011.

EYEWEAR PUBLISHING

EYEWEAR POETRY

MORGAN HARLOW MIDWEST RITUAL BURNING
KATE NOAKES CAPE TOWN
RICHARD LAMBERT NIGHT JOURNEY
SIMON JARVIS EIGHTEEN POEMS
ELSPETH SMITH DANGEROUS CAKES
CALEB KLACES BOTTLED AIR
GEORGE ELLIOTT CLARKE ILLICIT SONNETS
HANS VAN DE WAARSENBURG THE PAST IS NEVER DEAD
DAVID SHOOK OUR OBSIDIAN TONGUES
BARBARA MARSH TO THE BONEYARD
MARIELA GRIFFOR THE PSYCHIATRIST
DON SHARE UNION
SHEILA HILLIER HOTEL MOONMILK
FLOYD SKLOOT CLOSE READING
PENNY BOXALL SHIP OF THE LINE
MANDY KAHN MATH, HEAVEN, TIME
MARION MCCREADY TREE LANGUAGE
RUFO QUINTAVALLE WEATHER DERIVATIVES
SJ FOWLER THE ROTTWEILER'S GUIDE TO THE DOG OWNER
TEDI LÓPEZ MILLS DEATH ON RUA AUGUSTA
AGNIESZKA STUDZINSKA WHAT THINGS ARE
JEMMA BORG THE ILLUMINATED WORLD
KEIRAN GODDARD FOR THE CHORUS
COLETTE SENSIER SKINLESS
BENNO BARNARD A PUBLIC WOMAN
ANDREW SHIELDS THOMAS HARDY LISTENS TO LOUIS ARMSTRONG
JAN OWEN THE OFFHAND ANGEL
A.K. BLAKEMORE HUMBERT SUMMER
SEAN SINGER HONEY & SMOKE
RUTH STACEY QUEEN, JEWEL, MISTRESS

EYEWEAR PROSE

SUMIA SUKKAR THE BOY FROM ALEPPO WHO PAINTED THE WAR
ALFRED CORN MIRANDA'S BOOK

EYEWEAR LITERARY CRITICISM

MARK FORD THIS DIALOGUE OF ONE - WINNER OF THE 2015 PEGASUS AWARD FOR POETRY CRITICISM FROM THE POETRY FOUNDATION (CHICAGO, USA).